C000132582

SAIL OF THE CENTURY

Like the Thames in London; the Hudson in New York; the Danube in Vienna – all these iconic rivers create images of a place . . . of people, of cities and times.

Silhouetted against the darkening river, Pier Head visitors watch one of the ferries as she makes her way for the other side of the Mersey in October 1950

THE Mersey still makes waves, invokes dreams and – whether silent or angry – stirs wishes and hopes. Whether the ferries clinked their gates in Liverpool or Birkenhead or Seacombe. Further afield to Dublin, Belfast and the Isle of Man. And . . . back again. They are part of the landscape, the seascape. This is a log book full of love – pure nautical nostalgia. All aboard . . . we're ready to sail.

MERSEY FERRY TALES CREW

CAPTAIN Peter Grant
COXSWAIN Colin Hunt
NAVIGATOR Vicky Andrews
FIRST MATE Zoe Bevan
QUARTERMASTER Colin Harrison

Pictures courtesy of Liverpool Daily Post and Echo Archive, Mirrorpix
and National Museums Liverpool

Printed by PCP

Produced by Trinity Mirror Media
Business Development Director: Mark Dickinson, Executive Editor: Ken Rogers
Senior Editor: Steve Hanrahan, Editor: Paul Dove, Senior Art Editor: Rick Cooke
Trinity Mirror Media Marketing Executive: Claire Brown, Sales and Marketing Manager: Elizabeth Morgan
Sales and Marketing Assistant: Karen Cadman

CONTENTS

Trinity Mirror Media

© Trinity Mirror / Liverpool Daily Post & Echo

All Rights Reserved. No part of "Mersey Ferry Tales" may be reproduced, stored in a retrieval system, or transmitted in any form, or by any means, electronic, mechanical, photocopying, recording or otherwise without the prior permission in writing of the copyright holders, nor be otherwise circulated in any form of binding or cover other than in which it is published and without a similar condition being imposed on the subsequent publisher.

ISBN 9 781906802813

To buy prints of the images in this publication, or any photos in our fantastic maritime collection, log on to www.merseyshop.com/buyaphoto or call 0845 300 3021

HUSTLE AND BUSTLE

A busy day at Liverpool Landing Stage in 1957

A HISTORY OF THE FERRY

There's always been a ferry on the Mersey . . . well, almost.
Ferries have plied their way across the river for a thousand years.

THE Domesday Book of 1086 saw the first written record of a ferry on the Mersey at Seacombe.

The Benedictine monks at Birkenhead operated the first regular ferry service to the fishing point at Liverpool on market days.

They rowed across on market days, and offered to carry passengers.

In good weather this could take ninety minutes, otherwise (and more often) considerably longer.

The service was granted a royal charter by Edward III in 1330.

A charter was also granted to the Earl of Chester to run a service from Seacombe to Birkenhead – the beginnings of the Wallasey ferry service. The charge for a foot passenger in 1357 was a halfpenny.

A number of ferry services were operated by private families along the Wirral riverside, before the services were taken over by the corporation of Birkenhead and Wallasey.

By 1753, there were at least five different ferry points in Wirral at Ince, Carlett, The Rock, Birkenhead and Seacombe.

In 1750, Daniel Defoe recalled: "Here is a ferry over the Mersee. You land on the flat shore on the other side, and must be content to ride through the water for some length, not on horseback but on the shoulders of some Lancashire man who comes knee-deep to the boat's side to truss one up."

On the Liverpool side, the creation of the borough of Liverpool in 1207 confirmed a legal right of passages, where a toll could be collected for a ferry

A city at the crossroads of the world, Princes Landing Stage in 1872.

Egremont Pier circa 1890

service. Only the Burgesses were exempt from the charge.

In 1256 a £10 rent, taken as payment for a lease of all royal rights which included the ferry, was documented. Ownership of these ancient ferry rights passed in 1266 to Edmund, Earl of Lancaster.

But then in 1323 his son Thomas rebelled against King Edward II and the right of ferry transferred back to the Crown.

The Liverpool Right of Ferry passed into the ownership of the Molyneux family in 1537, where it remained for 220 years, until it was purchased by Liverpool Town Council.

The ferries ran their first steam-powered vessel, Etna, in 1815, which allowed the service to operate to a timetable. In 1830, when James Atherton bought the coastal area that he would develop into New Brighton, he also established the New Brighton Steam Packet Company.

By 1840, all ten services were operated by paddle steamers. The first diesel ferry was introduced over 100 years later in 1949. (Two years earlier the ferry service was the first in the world to use radar for safe navigation in fog.)

The last steam ferry, the Wallasey sailed in 1963.

Five years later, in 1968, the Wallasey and Birkenhead services merged into Mersey Ferries.

"The Benedictine monks at Birkenhead operated the first regular ferry service to the fishing point at Liverpool on market days"

PAST TIMES

Top, a view of the Mersey showing a ferry boat at the landing stage, circa 1890. Bottom, one of the first Mersey ferries, which only the well-to-do could afford to use

Rock Ferry in 1939

Crocus, the first coal-powered screw steamer,
introduced in 1884

NEW WORLD

Above, queues for New Brighton on the Royal iris in 1923 with a luggage boat and a CPR Mont liner in the background. Left, a char a banc leaves Woodside Ferry Terminal in the 1920s. The historic terminal, which is still recognisable today, opened in 1861 and was used to portray the port of Dover in the film Chariots of Fire

HELLO, GOODBYE

Above, the Liver Building is only two years old and the Cunard Building has yet to fill the gap. This was Liverpool waterfront in 1913. Names of the ferries at the landing stage are indiscernible but the one on the left could be the old Iris or Daffodil Left, an Austin crosses the river on a luggage boat back in March 1932

FIRST AMONG PIERS

Edwardian Sunday best on the Landing Stage in the early 20th century

The Channel Fleet, consisting of fourteen battleships and three cruisers, visits the Mersey in August 1907 as part of Liverpool's 700th birthday celebrations

Caption goes in here

Boarding the ferry from Seacombe
Landing Stage in May 1937

HEROES OF ZEEBRUGGE

Two famous Mersey Ferries went to war 93 years ago and came home, not only to nationwide acclaim, but also with a 'Royal' seal of approval.

*I*RIS and Daffodil each played remarkable support roles in the Royal Navy's attack on Zeebrugge on 23 April, 1918.

The German Navy had installed a lethal U-Boat base at the Belgian port which was posing a constant threat to Allied shipping in the English Channel. The plan was to sail right up to the port entrance and sink three old British cruisers, thus blocking the flow of traffic from the Base.

Eight Victoria Crosses would be won in what was one of the most daring raids of the First World War, and the Iris and the Daffodil were each granted the 'Royal' prefix to their names after sailing into the heart of a fierce battle, as part of the diversionary tactics alongside the mile-long Zeebrugge Mole.

The Iris and the Daffodil had long been renowned for ferrying passengers across the Mersey. They were extremely useful craft, each capable of carrying 1500 men if required. They drew little water, but possessed two disadvantages. Their low decks meant long storming ladders would be required to reach the parapet at Zeebrugge. Also, their steaming qualities were comparatively poor for the operation for which they were required.

Reaching their war destination was extremely different to the short daily crossings they were used to from Birkenhead and Wallasey to Liverpool.

Now they were being asked to make a 100 mile trek across open sea.

However, it was decided that the advantages of using these ferries, outweighed the disadvantages.

Both craft were designed to withstand heavy bumping alongside piers. Their draft was small and they were easy to handle. After minor alterations at Portsmouth, they set off for their new assignment, each adopting the titles of HMS, much to the amusement of the larger ships in the expedition.

READY FOR ACTION
The Iris during wartime

The first duty of Daffodil on arrival at the Mole was to push the much larger HMS Vindictive bodily alongside, enabling the latter to secure herself.

Daffodil was then to drop alongside Vindictive to enable her parties to climb over the larger vessel and up to the Mole.

The Iris was to go alongside the Mole ahead of Vindictive, to anchor and also secure to the latter, and to land her storming parties by means of ladders against the walls. In the event of Vindictive being sunk, Iris and Daffodil were to storm the Mole themselves and do everything possible to knock out the three-gun battery, or simply divert fire from the blockships. It should be noted that the enemy had up to 1,000 men on the Mole.

The Germans had heavy gun batteries along 21 miles of the coast, and smokescreens were required to mask those guns so the blockships and storming vessels could remain undiscovered until the last possible moment.

The convoy set out on a misty day with rain coming down in torrents. To help with their engines, Vindictive took Iris and Daffodil in tow, closely

followed by the blockships. Fast motor boats and two submarines were also taken in tow for the same reason.

Fifty minutes before midnight, the hawser being used to tow Iris and Daffodil suddenly parted. It was now too late to retake them in tow in the dark, murky conditions, and so the Mersey Ferries continued under their own power, although this meant they dropped behind.

However, their crews did a remarkable job and Iris was soon in position at the Mole, just 100 yards ahead of Vindictive exactly to plan. Daffodil then appeared and pushed her nose against Vindictive, again following the plan to the letter.

Some of the Daffodil crew, led by Lieut F.E. Chevallier, climbed up onto Vindictive and made their way to the Mole.

Iris dropped her anchor at the foot of the wall about five minutes after midnight, but the heavy swell was tossing her around like a cork, making the use of the parapet anchors extremely difficult.

After several failures to hook to the top of the wall, Lieut. Claude E. Hawkings, one of the officers of the storming party, ordered some men to hold up one of the scaling ladders. They could not lean it against the wall and so it was held vertically with no support at the top. Hawkings ran up it and leapt onto the Mole before the ladder was then smashed to pieces.

NEVER FORGET

The Mayor of Wallasey, Alderman Dingle, inspects a guard of honour on Prince's Landing Stage before a service in 1962 commemorating the anniversary of the storming of the Zeebrugge Mole during the First World War

He tried to fix the anchor, but came under immediate fire and while he tried to defend himself with a revolver, he was killed.

Lieut.-Commander George N. Bradford was in command of the storming party in Iris and his remit did not include securing the vessel. However, he climbed up the ship's derrick which carried a large parapet anchor.

The derrick was crashing onto the Mole with every roll of the ship, but he managed to jump to the wall, taking the anchor with him. He placed it in position, but was cut down by machine gun bullets and fell into the sea between Iris and the Mole. Gallant attempts to rescue his body failed.

It was later written that "one cannot conceive greater bravery than was shown by these two officers whose example will never be forgotten."

The anchor placed by Bradford suddenly slipped and now Iris drifted away from the Mole. Commander Valentine Gibbs, on the Iris, now decided to land his men across Vindictive.

He ordered the cable to be slipped and steamed around the stern of Daffodil to come alongside Vindictive.

The sight of these two Mersey Ferries in the thick of the action amongst much larger vessels was truly remarkable. Iris was told to run for it and did so under further heavy fire. She was hit by two large shells and the look-out house was destroyed, causing a fire on the upper deck. Gibbs was now mortally wounded, fearless to the end. His last words were for his crew and ship: "How are we doing?"

Most people thought Iris had been sunk, but this Mersey Ferry would come through this incredible firefight. Major C.E. Eagles, in command of the Marine storming parties on Iris, was also killed with many of his men. But Iris had played its part in assisting towards the safe passage of the blockships to the Zeebrugge Mole which was the main object of the exercise, severely reducing its effectiveness as a German Naval and Air Base.

Meanwhile Daffodil was extremely fortunate in having escaped serious damage, having been exposed to German battery fire for a full hour during which she kept Vindictive alongside the Mole.

She was able to proceed back to Dover. The two Mersey Ferries were acclaimed across Britain and they were renamed Royal Daffodil and Royal Iris, names their famous modern successors carry proudly to this day.

With thanks to 'The Blocking of Zeebrugge'
by Captain Alfred F B Carpenter
printed by Herbert Jenkins Ltd, London, 1922

The hole made in the Mole at Zeebrugge

BRAVE HEARTS

Right, map showing the attack on Zeebrugge on April 23, 1918. Opposite page, the Royal Iris, with a naval escort, sails for the Zeebrugge Remembrance Service on the Mersey in April 1973

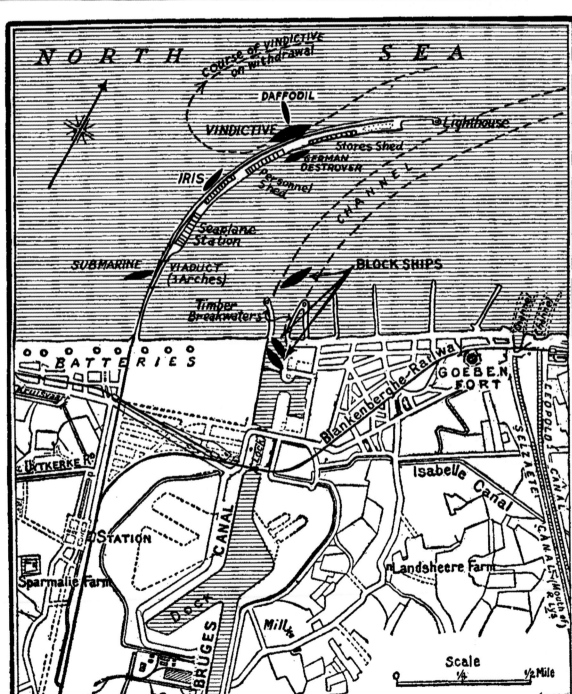

THE ROYAL FAMILY

For their role at Zeebrugge, King George V awarded the Daffodil and Iris the title of 'Royal' in recognition of their efforts. They remain the best loved of all the ferries.

FLOWER POWER

Left, the Royal Iris in 1968

DAFFODIL DAYS

Opposite page, passengers disembark from the Royal Daffodil at Liverpool Landing Stage, some of the many holidaymakers who went to New Brighton to enjoy the sunshine in April 1963, and main picture, the Royal Daffodil braves the waves in 1978

CROWNING GLORY

The name Iris began its long association with the Mersey Ferries in 1906, when the Wallasey Ferry Service acquired the Iris and the Daffodil from the Birkenhead service.

THE Wallasey service had always looked to local place names such as Overchurch and Woodchurch for its fleet, while Birkenhead had traditionally adopted flower names.

But the names were retained and the two ferries were to become the most famous of the fleet – the Iris particularly securing an affectionate place in the heart of the local community.

The Royal prefix was bestowed by King George V in recognition of the parts played by both the Iris and the Daffodil in the Zeebrugge raid. The legend was gathering pace.

In 1951, the third ferry to bear the name Royal Iris was delivered to Wallasey Corporation. Built by Denny's of Dumbarton and acquired at a cost of £400,000, she was the first diesel-electric ferryboat, and was intended to operate cruises, although she would also serve as a commuter ferry when required. She would be known locally as the Fish and Chip boat, the Love boat and even the booze boat.

In 1977, during Royal Jubilee celebrations, Queen Elizabeth II sailed on her. In the Eighties, Iris sailed to London to attend a Merseyside promotion in the Thames.

And when the QE2 visited the Mersey, in 1990, the Royal Iris served as a tender.

Shortly afterwards, she was retired from service. Sadly her non-working days were far from illustrious. After lying in Birkenhead Docks she was put up for sale. One of her engines failed as she left Birkenhead for Liverpool's Stanley Docks.

A number of different private commercial ventures were planned by subsequent owners, with a view to using her as a club ship and conference centre. But none were successful, and she now lies in tidal moorings in the Thames. She attracted the TV cameras again when she started to sink. A team of volunteers managed to board her and stop the leak.

As the reports of her sad fate reached Merseyside, a campaign to save her and return her to the Mersey was launched. But as yet, this mammoth task has yet to be achieved.

In 2002, following dry-docking and a refit, the Mountwood was returned to service, renamed as the Royal Iris of the Mersey.

FABULOUS FIFTIES

Top, the Royal Iris sets sail in August 1958.
Above, passengers in the cabin of the Iris in 1956

FULL SPEED AHEAD

The engine order telegraph, or EOT, on
the bridge of the Royal Iris

MAGIC MOMENTS

During his years as Liverpool ECHO features editor and marketing editor Arthur Johnson had numerous dealings with the Mersey Ferries and other vessels. Now a freelance Journalist, Arthur recalls some of those memories.

THE ferries, and in particular the Royal Iris, always had a special place in the hearts of Liverpool ECHO readers.

We only had to announce that we were chartering one of the 'little ships' – normally to raise money for one of our charities – and the bookings would come flooding in.

When we sailed out to the Mersey Bar to meet the QE2 when she first came to Liverpool it was special for me. As we set off with a packed ferry early on a glorious summer's morning, I felt a deep satisfaction.

Thousands upon thousands turned out to give the glorious vessel a special Merseyside welcome.

They lined the river banks all day long and sang along to Ferry Cross the Mersey playing from the ship, before she headed back to the Irish Sea to a farewell firework display, again accompanied by a ferry crowded with readers.

A few of us had a dream of the liners returning to the Mersey, but in all honesty that's all we thought – it was then a dream. The times we chartered the Royal Iris were particularly memorable. We had a number of 60s nights featuring Gerry and the Pacemakers, the Searchers, the Merseybeats and Billy Butler and Wally Scott.

Norman Thomas was the DJ for one sailing and was approached by a girl in her early twenties who asked if she could make a special announcement to surprise her 'fella' who was in the audience.

Norman agreed and she announced that she was pregnant.

After the baby was born we invited Norman back

onboard and the baby was christened on the bridge.

I'm proud of the fact that we chartered the Iris for her very last Mersey sailing on January 12, 1991.

I still have the commemorative ticket from the night. For £12.50 you got a five-hour cruise with live music from Kenny 'Sonny Webb' Johnson and Northwind, a disco and a supper of Scouse.

It was an emotional night with passengers remembering past cruises they had enjoyed on the 'Fish and Chip Boat' with the great names of the Merseybeat years playing live.

I was told on the bridge of the Iris that night I could have the ship for £1 – and just one snag, it would cost a fortune to make her properly seaworthy.

What a shame she sailed away from her home port the next day, never to return.

What an asset she would be to the river today. But we must be grateful that we still have the glorious ferries because at one stage it seemed they too would go.

PARTY TIME

Bookings would come flooding in for chartered trips, as these commemorative tickets show. Top, the Royal Iris is dwarfed by the QE2 on her visit to Liverpool in 2008

ALL DECKED UP
A sunny trip on board the Royal Iris in 1990

Today they play a vital part in Merseyside's booming tourism industry and Gerry Marsden's voice can be heard on every sailing.

The singer has become a close friend over the years and we even flew out to Australia with Liverpool FC's Brian Hall to found 'Scousers Down Under'.

I also arranged for him to arrive by ferry at the Pier Head when he received the Freedom of the City.

Years on, the River Mersey is cleaner than it has been for years, the River Festival will return and we have the International Pirate Muster Day.

Oh, and those cruise liners I dreamed of coming home are now a common sight at the Pier Head.

But, most importantly of all the ferries just keep sailing along . . . day in and day out.

As Gerry sings: "And here they'll stay."

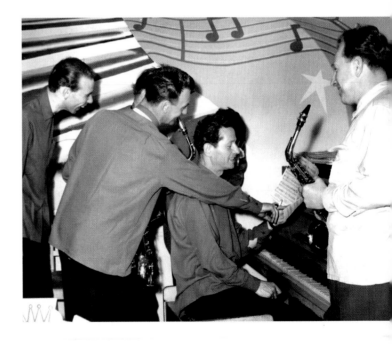

SAX APPEAL
In the swing of things with a jazz band

Overchurch takes to the water after her launch at Cammell Laird's yard in 1962

SISTERS OF MERSEY

Today's fleet of ferries have been plying the river for more than four decades. The Woodchurch took to the waters for the first time in 1960 and was renamed Snowdrop in 2004. Overchurch was the most recent Mersey ferry to be built, launched at Cammell Laird's yard in 1962. In November 1998, Overchurch went into dry dock in Manchester, where she was refurbished and given new engines. She emerged as the Royal Daffodil. The Mountwood, also built in 1960, underwent a major refit in 2002, and became the Royal Iris of the Mersey, perpetuating the memory of an illustrious predecessor.

In 1981, Woodchurch was withdrawn from operation for almost three years, due to cost cutting measures. She returned to service in 1983, after main engine repairs and a full repaint. She was renamed Snowdrop in 2004, to continue the line of Mersey ferries named after flowers

The Mountwood was used in the film 'Ferry Cross The Mersey'. In her early years she was an unreliable ferry, breaking down three times whilst crossing the river and had to anchor – her passengers had to be rescued by Woodchurch

FLOAT ON

Egremont Ferry
in 1933

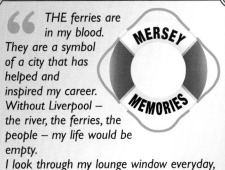

66 *THE ferries are in my blood. They are a symbol of a city that has helped and inspired my career. Without Liverpool – the river, the ferries, the people – my life would be empty.*

I look through my lounge window everyday, wishing someone would fix it, (only joking) and see the greatest waterfront in the world. The world – yes, I've been there, forget the rest. I wake up seeing the ferries swirl back and forth before I go to bed and then when I wake up in the morning. Now that's a comforting thing.

Sat in the Radio City Tower, I look over the rooftops and see the sun set over the Mersey, with those boats working away day in and day out, like the people of the city I love. That simply cannot … will not ever, ever be beaten. 99

PETE PRICE, RADIO PRESENTER

There she goes –
The Woodchurch
in 1973 and below,
flying the flag

THE ROCK AND ROLL YEARS

Thanks to Gerry Marsden – and a single song – the Mersey Ferry is the most famous boat in the world . . .

"JOIN the Ferry Cross the Mersey for fast and furious fun!" proclaims the film announcer as Gerry Marsden, glides down the gangway on a moped, guitar slung over his shoulder.

This 1965 celebration of the Mersey Sound was produced by Brian Epstein and featured, alongside Gerry Marsden and the Pacemakers, Cilla Black, The Fourmost, Julie Samuels, Jimmy Saville and, of course, the Mersey Ferry Mountwood.

With a simple storyline, and 14 musical numbers, the film captures the optimism and excitement of the Merseybeat scene. Stark and grainy images of industrial Liverpool contrast with the bright and

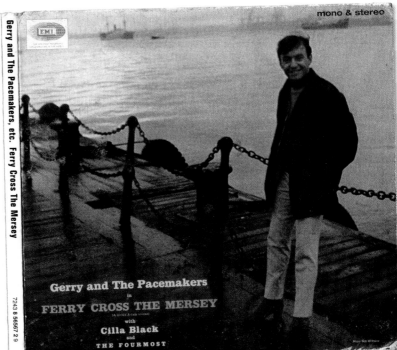

Gerry and The Pacemakers in
FERRY CROSS THE MERSEY
(A United Artists release)
with
Cilla Black
and
THE FOURMOST

1.	IT'S GONNA BE ALL RIGHT (Marsden) GERRY and THE PACEMAKERS	7. THIS THING CALLED LOVE (Marsden) GERRY and THE PACEMAKERS
2.	WHY OH WHY (Marsden) GERRY and THE PACEMAKERS	8. BABY YOU'RE SO GOOD TO ME (Marsden) GERRY and THE PACEMAKERS
3.	FALL IN LOVE (Marsden) GERRY and THE PACEMAKERS	9. I'LL WAIT FOR YOU (Marsden) GERRY and THE PACEMAKERS
4.	THINK ABOUT LOVE (Marsden) GERRY and THE PACEMAKERS	10. SHE'S THE ONLY GIRL FOR ME (Marsden) GERRY and THE PACEMAKERS
5.	I LOVE YOU TOO (Jacques-Ryan) THE FOURMOST	11. IS IT LOVE (Willis) CILLA BLACK
6.	ALL QUIET ON THE MERSEY FRONT (Martin) THE GEORGE MARTIN ORCHESTRA	12. FERRY CROSS THE MERSEY (Marsden) GERRY and THE PACEMAKERS

Produced for records by GEORGE MARTIN.
Cover Photography by Robert Whitaker.

lively young club goers packed into the Cavern.

But the enduring image has to be the apparently impromptu creation of the title song – Ferry Cross The Mersey – filmed on board the Mountwood.

"That's getting better, Chad, let me get my guitar," says Gerry, as Les Chadwick strums the opening chords. "Try a Latin American beat for that, Fred," says Chad to Freddie Marsden, who starts tapping out the rhythm on the back of a ferry seat, while Arthur finds his keyboard.

Gerry returns with the first line: "Life goes on day after day . . . " and the song flows out as freely as the river. It was so much simpler then.

MERSEY BEAT

Left, filming Ferry Cross the Mersey on the Mountwood in 1965.
Below, party time on the ferry

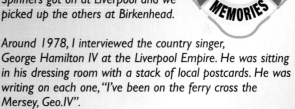

> *I DIDN'T go to any of the 60s Beat nights on the ferries but I did go to a folk night. I was amused that the performers were at the quayside with the rest of us. Two Spinners got on at Liverpool and we picked up the others at Birkenhead.*
>
> Around 1978, I interviewed the country singer, George Hamilton IV at the Liverpool Empire. He was sitting in his dressing room with a stack of local postcards. He was writing on each one, "I've been on the ferry cross the Mersey, Geo.IV".
>
> When Gerry Marsden was given the freedom of the ferries by the then Lord Mayor Steve Rotherham, there was a short ceremony aboard the boat and he then sang his famous song. It was a regular journey and so there were tourists on board. They may well have thought, "Poor man. He was once a big star and now he's singing 'Ferry Cross The Mersey' on the boat for a living."
>
> The Liverpool singer, Lita Roza stipulated in her will that her ashes should be scattered on the Mersey and that happened in 2008. It was as though she was saying, "No matter what happens to me, I belong here." Last year, I attended the scattering of Clinton Ford's ashes on the Mersey. It was a joyous occasion as the Merseysippi Jazz Band and many of his friends were there. It seemed a wonderful way to say goodbye.
>
> I'm hoping that my last journey will be on the ferry "and here I'll stay." By the way, don't worry about ashes blowing into your face – the considerate captain stops halfway and turns the ferry into the wind! "
>
> *SPENCER LEIGH, BBC RADIO MERSEYSIDE*

MERSEY MEMORIES

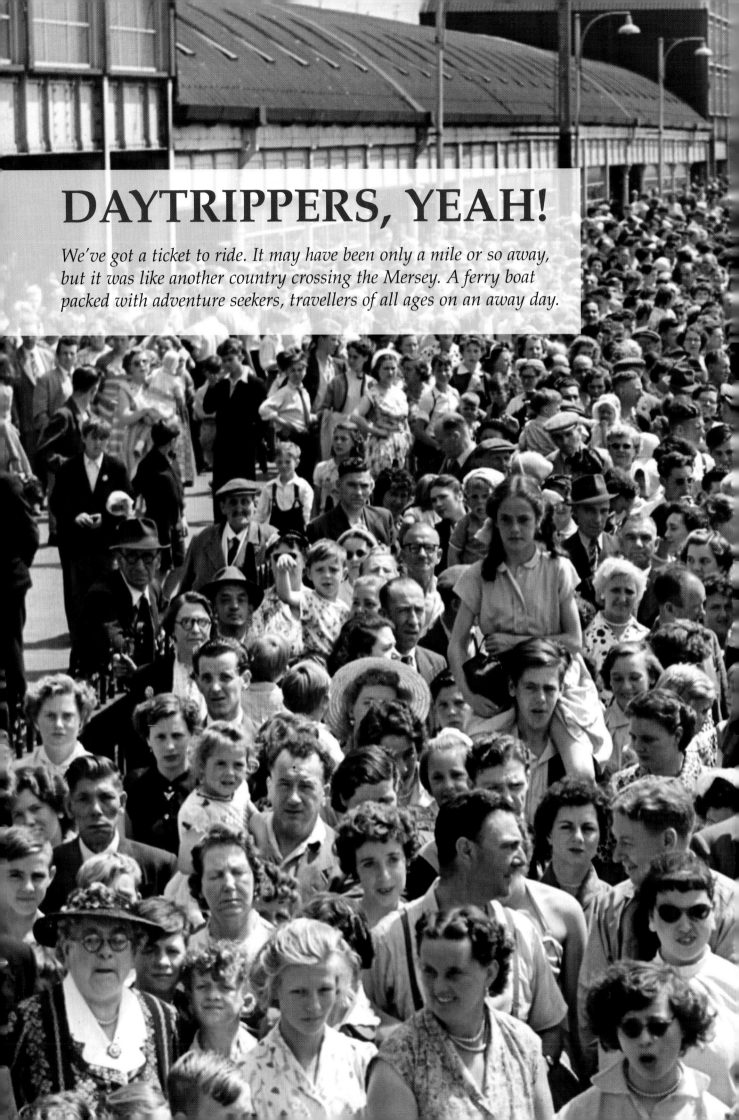

DAYTRIPPERS, YEAH!

We've got a ticket to ride. It may have been only a mile or so away, but it was like another country crossing the Mersey. A ferry boat packed with adventure seekers, travellers of all ages on an away day.

> IN the years that go drifting by I recall the ferries in the 40s and 50s.
> On Saturday I would meet friends from work and go to the Pier Head for a boat over to New Brighton Tower for the dancing.
> The boys from West Kirby RAF camp would be there and we would all dance the night away to the Bill Gregson band. All too soon it was over and time to go and get the ferry back to Liverpool. We would go on the top deck and dance all the way.
> The great deck hands would give us a cheery wave with a "See you next week, girls!"

MRS EVELYN F SHACKLADY, AINTREE

HAPPY HOLIDAYS

Above, youngsters celebrate the Easter break in 1962. Right, passengers disembark at New Brighton in 1966

GARDEN STATE

A special ferry service is launched in 1984 for visitors to the International Garden Festival. The MV Overchurch sailed in red, white and blue colours from the Pier Head via Woodside and then on to Otterspool close to the festival site. The service was given a sparkling send off by Bunty Campbell, wife of former Ferries Manager Hugh Campbell; Councillor David Langton; Captain Alan Jones; Gaynor Bell from Tuebrook and Jan Eedle from Crosby

AMERICAN EXPRESS

Stateside visitors get snap happy on the Mersey Ferry in 1982

THE VOICE OF THE FERRY

Eithne Browne, actor and theatre star, now plays her own part in the famous waterfront's history, as one of the 'voices' of the Mersey Ferries.

FOR Eithne Browne, the intoxicating sights, sounds and smells of Liverpool's docks are more than just the evocative stuff of childhood memories. They're in her blood.

With her dad, a ship's captain, her grandad a docker and her other grandparents running a Dock Road pub, she grew up captivated by the magic of the Mersey. Now, the actress who became a familiar face to millions as Brookside's Chrissie Rodgers, is heard by hundreds of thousands of visitors who make the Mersey Ferry crossing each year, sharing the secrets of the river and its enduring appeal.

"I loved the ferries when I was younger," she remembers. "I was one of seven children and we always used to go down to the Pier Head. I suppose it was a busman's holiday for my dad but we loved it. We'd spend hours fascinated by the ships, just sitting looking at everything going on.

"I was very honoured to be asked to be the voice of the ferry. I am a born and bred Liverpudlian, but there are visitors from all over the world – seeing this iconic attraction and wanting to know and hear more. So it can't be too Scouse – the accent and tone have to be just right. You have to make it crystal clear and I have since had so many wonderful memories when people have been on board and come over and said: 'Is that you over the speakers?'

"I am particularly proud that my late dad heard it and loved it. Friends, to this day, tell me they enjoy it too and find it so informative and educational."

"The only thing is people do get confused and expect to see me, sitting with a microphone in a blue and yellow Mersey Ferries sweater on every crossing!"

Eithne says the ferries are always evolving and changing.

"There's a little piece of me in the ferries now. I'm very happy that I've contributed a small part to its ongoing history. Like the city and like the river – everything changes. I have been back to add bits and delete things and there's a male voice too.

"But for me it's more than a great element in my career to be talking to global visitors you will never meet but you have left your mark on them.

"It's lovely being remembered as a voice of the ferry."

The Royal Iris sets sail from Seacombe

SEASIDE ESCAPE

Sun and sandcastles, the ferris wheel, the fairground. Fish and chips, lemonade and candy floss. Happy days at New Brighton in the 1960s

JOY RIDE

Wallasey's Royal Iris bus in 1970

WE ARE WAITING IN LINES

A Short Story

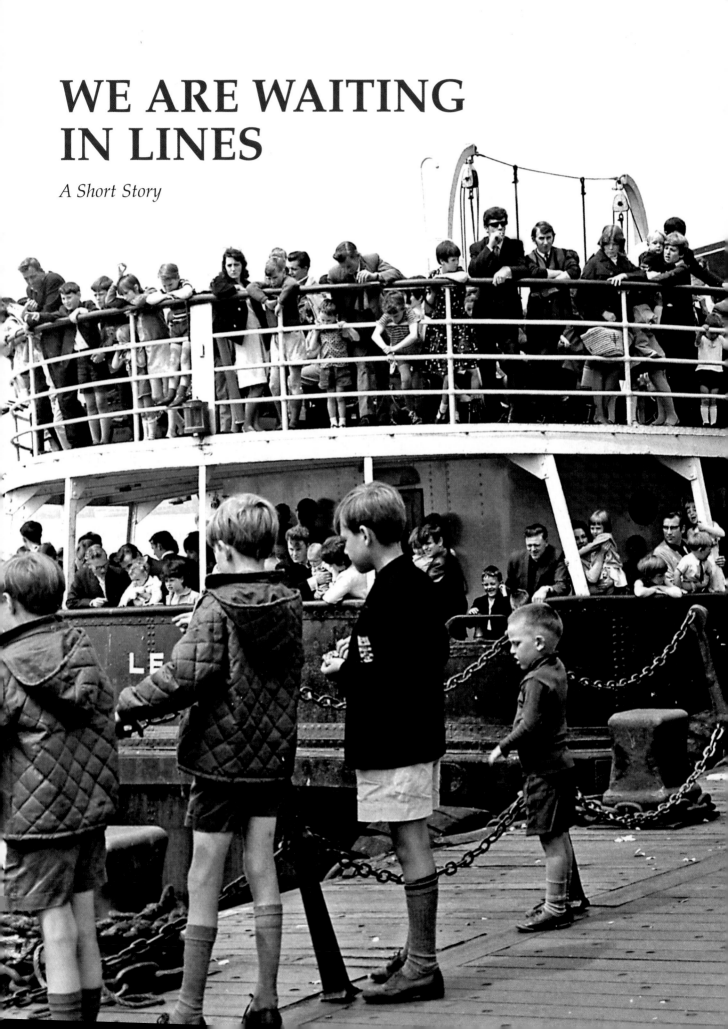

By Cathy Roberts, Storyteller

QUIETLY giggling – some through nerves but most through excitement, as the landing stage gently rises and falls.

Then Ralphie spots it coming, and the line surges like horses at the start of the National.

With precisely measured control, Mrs Taylor calls the only name she needs to – Ralphie Vaughan – and both lines stand to attention.

The engines roar as the river foams and the tyres along the landing stage creak and squeak, until finally the gangplank lowers like a drawbridge, and we run. Though we shouldn't, we run ahead and up the steps in the great rush to the upper deck. Bursting through the doorway, the wind slaps you back and you lick the sea salt from your lips. There are loads of seats but the whole class is making for the front ones. Except for Ralphie and Jimmy, who've already vanished off to plan mutiny.

I run my hand along the icy cold rail towards the stern and pull myself right up to the edge of the deck. Mrs Taylor has Ralphie under surveillance. Julie and Paula and the two Annes are up the front end. Nobody's watching me. I lean over the rail as far as I dare and stare down at the foaming wake. I could be anywhere. I can hear Mrs Taylor, faintly, talking about smugglers caves. But as I stare into the glistening waves, time stands still. I keep looking down, and then I see it – a face looking back at me. Clear as daylight – a beautiful face, with long flowing hair, white like the waves. I hold my breath. Then she turns and a huge fish tail bursts through the waves, splashing me in the face. Then it disappears. I gasp, but can't speak. A hand on my shoulder pulls me firmly away from the rail.

I look up at Mrs Taylor.

"Did you see it?"

But all she said was "Ralphie Vaughan!" as the eyes in the back of her head pinpointed the mutineers sneaking out of bounds.

ADVENTURE LAND

The Leasowe proves an exciting place for youngsters in the 1960s

MANX TALES

Part of the enchantment of the Isle of Man was travelling by sea – the ships seemed magical, the saloons with their panelling and highly-polished brass, the stewards in their white jackets with dickie-bow ties and the officers in their traditional uniforms...

THE Isle of Man Steam Packet Company is the oldest continually operating passenger shipping company in the world.

The first packet boat service was established two years after the Crown purchased the island from the Atholl family, in 1765.

Britain had suffered considerable loss of revenue through the smuggling trade that had thrived on the island, and as a result, a garrison of Redcoats was established. The packet boat service operated from Whitehaven to Douglas for the benefit of the garrison. The first steam service to call at the Island, en route from Liverpool to Greenock, established Douglas as a port of call. The service quickly attracted competition in the form of the St George Steam Packet Company of Liverpool, offering a service from Liverpool, via Douglas, to Glasgow.

Unsurprisingly, the islanders began to feel they warranted their own Steam Packet Company.

An enterprising Manxman named Cosnahan acquired the steamer Victory in 1926, and attempted to operate a service from Liverpool to Douglas. ➤

BOAT SHOW

A scene on the Liverpool Landing Stage in October 1957 shows the Isle of Man steamer Mona's Isle leaving with weekend holidaymakers. A Cunard White Star liner is returning after her last holiday cruise of the season. Opposite page, boarding the Isle of Man Steam Packet Company's Lady of Mann in July 1960

However his bid to syndicate shares in the business proved unsuccessful and it wasn't until a meeting was held in December 1829, that the required commitment was achieved. A committee was formed to examine the cost of purchasing and running a steamer, and within six months the Isle of Man Steam Packet Company was established.

During the Great War, 11 out of 15 vessels were requisitioned by the Admiralty, with four being lost and three held by the government.

The Manxman was probably the first vessel to be converted to an aircraft carrier using Sopwith Pup planes. In the Second World War, the company lost four of its 10 best ships through requisitioning.

It also provided valiant service at Dunkirk, with the Mona's Isle being the first vessel to leave Dover and complete the round trip during the evacuation.

Eight of the company's ships took part in the operation, rescuing 24,699 British troops (equivalent to one in every fourteen of the lives saved.)

Since then the service has continued to operate, as the Isle of Man soon became a popular holiday destination.

The TT races, in late spring, sees the service ferrying 35,000 passengers, plus approximately 14,000 motorbikes. (Over 36,000 pints of beer are sold during the crossing, not to mention the 40,000 sandwiches, nine tonnes of chips and 200 cups of tea.)

With a fast Seacat service, or a more traditional Ben-My-Chree, the company continues to carry over 600,000 passengers each year.

And not a smuggler in sight.

BREAK AWAY

Right, The Isle of Man steamer Ben-My-Chree disgorging thousands of holidaymakers returning from the TT races week in the 1950s. Below, the scene at the Pier Head in 1956 as crowds queue for the boat

Mirrorpix

THE SHUFFLE BOAT

THEY'VE been there as long as we can remember, but open up the old box marked ferries somewhere in the memory vault, blow off the dust, lift the lid, and let the childhood magic escape.

The smell. That heady mixture of marine diesel, hot metal and salt water rising up in warm draughts from the engine room hatch, sometimes mixed with cigarette smoke from the engineer leaning on the rail taking a breather from the heat below.

But the journey begins before then, the echo of feet as you run down the ramp to the landing stage, or if the weather's good the exhilaration of the outside walkway.

Swinging on the chains you could watch your ferry's curved approach, hear the shudder of the engines as it slows to a stop and eases into the stage.

The gentle rocking under your feet and squeals of protest from the tyres as they bounced the ferry into position were like a berth announcement. The crewman snakes over the thin line which the stagehand uses to haul in the heavy hemp mooring

It's easy to take the ferries for granted, writes archivist and author Colin Hunt. They're as much a part of the landscape as the river itself, but most of us never even notice or use them.

rope and winds it around the cast iron bollard. The rumble of the gate being pushed across and the clatter and bang as the gangways come down.

Straight on board and up to the top deck to bag a speck at the bow. All very different from the Monday to Friday commuter crossings when workers packed into the saloons to read their morning papers, or took to the breezy upper deck where, with Trilbies and Homburgs wedged over their Brylcreemed heads, they walked the walk and talked the talk in the daily ritual of the anti-clockwise promenade.

There were other ferry

The 487-ton Birkenhead ferry steamer Thurstaston (pictured here in 1961) was launched in 1930 from Cammell Laird's shipyards. She was coal-fired with a speed of about 11 knots and accommodation for 1,433 passengers

*THE CAVERN PRESENTS
A RIVERBOAT
SHUFFLE
FRIDAY. 25TH AUG. 1961.
ABOARD THE
" M.V. ROYAL IRIS "
WITH
MR.
ACKER BILK'S
PARAMOUNT JAZZ BAND
and THE BEATLES
BOAT SAILS AT 7.45 P.M.
FROM LIVERPOOL LANDING STAGE
RETURNING AT 11.0 P.M.
Tickets
8|6

rides too, the best being the North Wales steamer to Llandudno and Beaumaris. School holidays with bikes and camping gear onto the St Tudno or St Seiriol along the coast to Ynys Mon, an easy escape from the city to beautiful beaches, clear seas, generous Welsh girls and Welsh rain.

The return journey was often grim, cold, soaked through, and the sight of the grey sulphurous cloud of thousands of coal fires and factory chimneys on the horizon that signalled we were nearly home would send your heart into your boots.

"Good people, you're invited tonight/ To the Riverboat Shuffle!/ Good people we got rhythm tonight/ At the Riverboat Shuffle!"

The lyrics of Hoagy Carmichael's 1924 tribute to the Mississippi riverboat jazz bands could easily be applied to the Merseysippi Jazz Band and the other bands that played on the Royal Iris in the 50s.

Although its bulbous nose, dummy funnel and slab sided yellow and green superstructure made it about as stylish as a pink Vauxhall Cresta, the warm memories of that floating dance hall will always remain. The vibration of the heavy bass amps combined with the throb of the engines created a sensation like no other.

The rejuvenating blast of fresh air as you came up on deck from the dance hall heat.

The salty stolen kisses as the cries of seagulls, their silhouettes white against the dark brooding skies, were swept away on the Mersey wind. The memories form a heady cocktail, a toast to lost youth.

The ferries are part of the DNA of all Merseysiders. We should make it a condition of residence that each one of us rides the ferry at least once a year to keep the magic of the Mersey alive in our hearts and souls.

SWEPT AWAY DAYS

Top, St Seiriol approaches Llandudno Pier in May 1959. St Seiriol was built by Fairfields in 1931, as a smaller second ship to assist St Tudno and operate excursions. Bottom, the scene on an April evening in 1963 as trippers make their way to the buses at the Pier Head

"The ferries are the
lifeblood of all
Merseysiders. We should
all ride the ferry at least
once a year to keep the
magic of the Mersey alive
in our hearts and souls"

MERSEY MEMORIES

" I LOVE the ferries. I went on them as a kid en route to see my relatives. It's great that people can have day break cruises up and down the Mersey and see the wild life – the birds and scenery. There's no better trip to see the Iron Men on Crosby Beach than from the ferry. You can join me and Mersey River Pilot manager Stuart Wood on the Mersey Ferries' charters on trips during the summer. The cruises show off the well-loved landmarks and hidden gems of the River Mersey. In the past we have raised money for Clatterbridge Hospital. The ferries and river are seen like never before. "

ANDY BALL, JOURNALIST & BROADCASTER

LANDING STAGE

By Peter Grant

MUM, Mum, tell me,
Where do the ferries go at night?
They work so hard,
All day, is it throughout the night?
Do they cuddle and sleep?
Have they . . . Mum, a special secret to keep?
While I'm at school,
All day they are going back and forth,
Swirling away.
I'm sorry, Mum (got to say),
Sagged off Maths and French . . . yesterday.
Walked down to the Pier Head,
Me and 'Gossy Maloo'.
She hates that nickname,
And slapped me.
Cried out loud: "I hate you."

I said: "C'mon Gossy,
"Look look, the boats must be here."
She said: "OK, but don't dare flick my ear."
Gossy said: "I've got to get home,"
I said: "Fine, but one more hour,
don't leave me alone."
She said: "Where are they, then?
"Ha, ha too late – no boat show."
I said: "Shush! I don't know."
But she whispered: "Yer Mum knows,
where they really go."
The ferries weren't there . . . it just wasn't fair.

If ships could talk, what tales of the Mersey could be told? The Mountwood and Claughton (Birkenhead ferry fleet) in 1960

I said: "Gossy" (she's only got one good
eye you see, so she can only half see)
I said: "Time then we have to fly."
I sighed (I often do): "Just me and you,
Gossy.
"Them and us."
Luckily, we caught the last bus.
Said goodbye to Gossy and we both
went home.
Would have rang her, but in those days,
no one had invented the mobile phone.
Got in, sheltered along by a street lamp-
light.
I said, "Mum . . . where do ferries go at
night?"
She said: "Here's your milk.

"They turn up, Luv, again tomorrow
morning,
"At daylight – now, stop that yawning."
I asked: "Do they go to a ferry home for
rest?
"A sort of light house – a cosy sea bed
and breakfast?
"Mum, like sweets, don't they need
some sort of fuel?
"Cos . . . cos,
"I want to bring them chocolate
tomorrow,
"Please, before I go to school."

PASSPORT TO PARADISE

By Tony Maudsley, Kirkby-born actor and Hollywood star

I WAS about 12 years old when Merseyrail first introduced its 'SAVEAWAY' ticket in the early 1980s.

For about 30p, kids were suddenly given a passport to the whole of Merseyside for what, even then, seemed like no cost at all. It was a while before I realised that not only could kids access all of the train and bus routes, but could also use the ferry. A free ride on a boat! Sounded good to me. And what an expedition!

I got a train to Moorfields and from there made my way down to the Pier Head. I looked at the expansive river before me as I'd done many times before and in the distance could see a land that I'd never been to before. Wirral. (Well I thought I'd never been there before, until my Dad set me straight and told me I'd been there loads of times.) It hadn't quite registered that the place on the other end of the Mersey Tunnel was the same place as on the other side of the river. Geography was never my strong point.

I made my way down to the quayside and there was the ferry, awaiting my arrival, like it knew I was coming. I climbed aboard and immediately headed upstairs to the open deck. I remember it was raining loads but that's where I wanted to sit. There'd be no point otherwise. The wooden benches were wet but once the rain had soaked through to my backside and warmed up against my skin, it was fine.

NIGHT LIGHT

The Three Graces elegantly define the skyline in 1967
Mirrorpix

I remember feeling so full of anticipation of all of the exciting things that I was going to see on the other side.

There was a blast of an ear splitting bass baritone foghorn and we were off. The vessel bounced on and off the quayside a few times and I worried that it might sink but eventually it found its way to the open water and set off to . . . well, I wasn't sure, but the other side at least.

To be honest, the sailing was disappointingly short lived and before I knew it a big burley Scouse ferryman bellowed that we'd arrived in Seacombe.

Seacombe? Never heard of it. I followed the other passengers and got off to discover this unfamiliar territory. A bit scared, I turned around and got straight back on the boat.

Slightly ashamed at my own lack of adventure, I sat back down on the open deck, still in the pouring rain, still with a wet arse, as the foghorn sounded and the ferry bounced free into the open water.

Only this time, spread out in front of me, like the shot of New York City at the start of Kojak, was Liverpool. Beautifully long, wide, vast, warm and familiar in a panoramic snapshot that I'd never seen before. It was just the same dirty old city that I'd known all my life but this time it took my breath away.

The cathedrals, the Liver Buildings, the Tower Restaurant, that clock with all the faces that I only ever saw when the train left Sandhills. All of it looking resplendent and majestic despite the rain, and suddenly it was all worthwhile.

TIME AND TIDE

Top, a boisterous autumn high tide at Seacombe Ferry Terminal in September 1963. Left, crowds at the Pier Head in 1958

> *I cast my mind back to those magical childhood days. The ferries to me back then were galleons; tall ships, huge ocean-going liners when I was a kid. I sailed away with my imagination. We would go down there and we would 'bunk on' and hide — real cheeky stowaways.*
>
> *But what adventures! We didn't want to get off the gangplank. We were sailing the high seas years before Johnny Depp in Pirates of the Caribbean! When I was asked to be part of International Pirate Day, meeting and greeting passengers on the ferries, I said "Ooh aaghh." I finally got to command my own ship for the day in full pirate costume. The Mersey, the ferries and me — no, you can't separate them.*

MERSEY MEMORIES

DEAN SULLIVAN, TV AND STAGE STAR

READY FOR BUSINESS

A panorama across the Mersey towards Seacombe in 1965. Below, before the Mersey Tunnel opened in 1934 the only way for vehicles to cross the Mersey was on the luggage boats. This is a typical queue for the luggage boats in 1932. The luggage boat service to Woodside continued until 1941, the Seacombe service finished in 1947

MEMORIES OF A BOAT LAD

By Dave Gilbertson

*I*T was May 1975, I was a 16-year-old Huyton lad and had just left school – I had applied to join the Royal Navy and was waiting for my joining instructions as Marine Engineer.

One night as usual my mates and I were hanging around outside the local 'Offy', when out of the blue me mate Snip shouted: "I'm off down to the Pier Head tomorrow, me uncle works on the Isle of Man Boats, anyone fancy coming down with me to see if we can get a job?"

I thought why not, nothing to lose. At eight o'clock the next morning we were on the H8 bus bound for the Pier Head. By ten o'clock the same morning we were aboard the MV Mona's Queen bound for the Isle of Man.

I was put to work in the pantry: duties, washing the dishes, pots and pans from the restaurant and galley. Snip's duties: collecting and washing cups, saucers and plates from the decks and the lounges.

At around eight o'clock the same evening the MV Mona's Queen had returned to the Pier Head, we were then to do a 'light trip' (no passengers) back to The Douglas. Well about eight weeks passed before I was to make it home, I had to jump the bus home between sailings to collect some more clothes.

I had become one of the Boat Lads (a name given to the Liverpool lads who worked on the boats by the Manx locals). I remained a Boat Lad for 12 long months, doing at least two trips a day, with hundreds of people every day.

I eventually joined the Royal Navy in the latter half of 1976.

I'm now happily married and living in Whiston with my family. My mate Snip?

Unfortunately he became violently sea sick and was a Boat Lad for . . . just over a week.

He now works in the construction industry. Oh, and for the last 24 years he's been my brother-in-law!

ROUND OUR WAY

The Pier head in 1961

MAKING WAVES

Strong and sturdy, the ferries are known for their ability to operate whatever the weather, but they've had their share of turbulent times – on and off-land.

The high tide driven by strong winds is a source of fascination for schoolboys and bus crews alike

LEAD KINDLY LIGHT

Fog on the Mersey and the scene at Liverpool
Landing Stage as a ferry is guided in by the
light of oil flares in December 1960

COLD FRONT

A solitary figure on the bridge braves
the elements on a midwinter crossing

Ferried away from a stranded Royal Daffodil II
in September 1967

WASHOUT

Water washes over
George's Parade in
January 1976.

FREE SPEECH

The Hyde Park Corner of Liverpool. Free expression of speech has long been a feature at Liverpool Pier Head. The picture shows two orators, on their four-legged stools, practising their art in 1965

PEOPLE POWER

Councillor J Newton (left) collects signatures for a petition against the withdrawal of the New Brighton Ferry in November 1964

LIFESAVER IS LOCAL HERO

Ted Towey worked as a deckhand on the Birkenhead ferries from 1954 to 1962, a career that started just after leaving school.

IN his early years at sea, aged just 17, on four separate occasions he dived into the Mersey at night, jumping into the icy cold waters to rescue people.

He helped to rescue a man in January 1963 and in 1960 helped to rescue a woman from the river, on both occasions from a boat.

Another time he rescued two men, one woman and a dog called Spotty, returning them all to the landing stage. For saving the humans he received a medal and a certificate. In the case of the dog he received a five shilling postal order from its pensioner owners.

In 1964, Ted made the news with another daring rescue, diving into the river to save Thomas Whelan. Ted, now aged 70, still lives in Birkenhead.

20th April, 1964

FERRY MAN'S BRAVERY REWARDED

A FERRY boat crewman's bravery in diving in the Mersey to rescue a passenger who had disappeared overboard was rewarded at a ceremony at Birkenhead Town Hall.

The Mayor, Alderman John H Roberts, presented to Seaman Edward Towey of Deakin Street, Birkenhead, the Bronze Marine Medal of the Liverpool Shipwreck and Humane Society.

Making the presentation, the Mayor said that at 11.25pm on April 11 a passenger disappeared over the starboard side of a corporation ferry boat.

The Mayor said: "Working as I do for the Mersey Docks and Harbour Board I know the difficulties of anyone who goes in the water, particularly at this time of the evening when the tide is on the ebb.

"What seaman Towey did was most meritorious. One of the greatest things a man can do is to run over into the swift running tide to pull another person out."

Alderman Horace D Shakeshaft, deputy chairman of the Transport Committee, said that however far back one went in the history of the ferries service there were always men who had been ready to go overboard to rescue people irrespective of the tide or the weather.

"It is grand to find such employees in our service."

Ice floes in the Mersey in January 1973 as a ferry leaves for Liverpool

LIFEBLOOD OF THE CITY

The discovery of a family tragedy in the River Mersey made a strong affinity with the ferries all the more poignant, writes journalist and author Ken Rogers.

THE Mersey Ferries have been an integral part of my life. As a young boy, I journeyed on them to the seaside paradise of New Brighton.

As a teenager, (pictured left) I played on the famous Royal Iris as a member of a local pop group. As an adult, I travelled to work every day using the ferries as a very special mode of transport. It's not surprising that the ferries have always had a fatal fascination for me.

However, I didn't realise the true relevance of those words until last summer as I researched my book 'The Lost Tribe of Everton & Scottie Road' and discovered that my Great Grandmother, Margaret Rogers, was actually reported missing off a ferry in April, 1921.

Aged 63, she was eventually recovered from under the Woodside Landing Stage and while the subsequent inquest declared an 'Open Verdict', it was clear that she had struggled to come to terms with a series of First World War family tragedies relating to her sons.

So having unearthed this shocking fact, is it still possible for me to look at the ferries in anything

MORNING CALL

Above, passengers brave the top deck of the ferry in 1964.
Right, catching up on the day's news on the way to work

Crowds pass from the
New Brighton ferry in 1952

river view, all for the price of a return ticket. The return journey is via Woodside and then Seacombe. Back in the 1970s, I used to take the ferry to work every single day from Birkenhead to Liverpool, one of 7 million passengers a year at that time.

Of course, back in the 1950s, the number was as high as 30 million. At this time, the ferry meant only one thing to me, a child's journey to a Wirral seaside resort that I could see every day from our street, high on Everton's famous ridge – the incredible New Brighton with its outdoor and indoor fairs that hypnotically called out to every kid on Merseyside, a packed beach with its deckchairs and donkeys, and an Art Deco Lido with its circular open air swimming pool.

The ferries to New Brighton would eventually stop in 1971 when the famous pier was demolished. The new Wallasey Tunnel became the revised route to New Brighton. It seemed to be the beginning of the end for the ferries as a genuinely viable transport option, but these days the ferries are as big an attraction to a worldwide visitor audience as the Liver Building, the Albert Dock or the Mathew Street Beatles Quarter.

Merseytravel has inspired a life-saving ferry revival. All we need now is for the New Brighton Pier and Tower Ballroom to be rebuilt and everything will be right with the world once more!

other than a tragic way ahead of the 90th anniversary of her death? The fact is, I can never get away from the ferries nor will I ever want to. They have been an eventful, magical part of my life. Even as I write this, looking down on the famous river from the Liverpool ECHO building in Old Hall Street, a ferry is breaking through the waves heading directly towards me, doing what she does best – providing one of the most spectacular journeys to work in the whole world.

These days, the ferry as a 'work horse' sails from Merseytravel's Seacombe terminal to the Pier Head, including free parking, free coffee and a world-class

THE IRISH CONNECTION

In an era when air-travel was beginning to make inroads, the B+I line car ferries, with their first-class accommodation, were still real ships with serious tonnage.

P & O ferries in Princes Dock in 1981

HE British and Irish Steam Packet Company had been formed in 1936, with investors that included Arthur Guinness and James Jameson.

Their first ships were wooden paddle steamers, but they soon became one of the first companies to invest in propeller driven ships. In 1917, the Liverpool Shipping company, which was taken over by the Kylsant Royal Mail Company, was renamed Coastlines. By the end of that year Coastlines owned all the shares in the B+I Line.

1929 saw the arrival of the Lady Munster for the Dublin – Liverpool route, soon to be joined by the

Lady Connaught and the Lady Leinster, which started the long association of vessels bearing these names with Liverpool.

The war years saw the removal of the fleet from its regular service, despite the ships being Irish registered. Coastlines was a British company and committed its ships to the war effort. Leinster became a hospital ship, then a troop carrier, while Munster hit a mine not far from the Liverpool Bar, in 1940. The company rebuilt its fleet, but advances in faster transportation through the Fifties and Sixties left the company struggling. The Irish Government

took over the company in 1965, making Coastlines truly Irish. Through the appointment of a new board of directors, the roll-on roll-off ferries were acquired, with the new Munster making her first sail on May 15, 1968, with a journey time three hours faster than her predecessors. The Leinster joined soon after.

The company briefly ran a jetfoil service, but its high running costs and poor performance in high seas proved impractical.

Throughout the 1980s losses continued to mount, and in January 6, 1988, the MV Connaught made the last B+I sailing between Liverpool and Dublin ending 152 years of service.

JET SET

Top, the B+I ferry MV Leinster passes Howth Head in Dublin on one of her regular sailings from Dublin to Liverpool in 1980. Above, the Jetfoil has its first trials on the River Mersey in 1980, ready for the start of a regular Dublin service

IN pre-easyJet and Ryanair days there was only one route from Liverpool to Ireland for those on a restricted budget and, before stabilisers made ferry crossings much smoother, journeys could be more of an endurance test than a joy.

My introduction to the Liverpool – Dublin link was in the late 1980s, when weekend ferries were chocka with Irish football fans heading to Liverpool, and the English off for a Guinness-fuelled weekend in Dublin's fair city. As we boarded for the evening crossing the skies were leaden and growing ominously heavier. The airline-style seating and creature comforts of today's vessels were still light years away, so choice was in short supply for the several hours that stretched ahead of us. Space in the bar was at a premium as the football songs began to ring out and the 'black stuff' flowed, so the only alternative was the galley, situated deep, deep within the bow.

As we ploughed further into the Irish Sea the rising wind and driving rain began to take effect as the ship was tossed from wave to wave, punctuated by the inevitable plunge into the oncoming spume that produced a resounding, thunderous, shuddering crack against the bow plates just inches away.

Even now I can still visualise that galley, silenced by a spreading, nervous trepidation as the storm worsened, or the sheer exhaustion of those who had succumbed to sporadic bouts of wretching as the ship lurched from side to side.

And although I don't consider myself especially religious, by God, I prayed that night!

NEIL HODGSON, BUSINESS JOURNALIST

In 1968 the B+I Line introduced their 'Motorway' service between Liverpool and Dublin, with the arrival of the new Munster, seen here in 1973

Millions of people used the old Runcorn-Widnes Transporter Bridge (seen here in 1961) to cross the Mersey and Manchester ship canal for over 50 years

LIFE GOES ON DAY AFTER DAY...

The Mersey still makes waves, invokes dreams and – whether silent or angry – stirs wishes and hopes. The ferries took people to work and brought them home. At weekends they took families, lovers and dreamers away on trips . . . and they will never retire. A part of all our lives, like loyal friends and a floating fixture of our heritage.

ROPE & GLORY

Three men in a boat – crew working on a ferry in 1926

PAPER TRAIL

Commuters manage to get a seat on the river rush hour in the late Fifties

The ferry from Liverpool emerges from a fog-shrouded
river at Woodside on an August morning in 1972

MERSEY MEMORIES

> TOWARDS the end of the Second World War I used to go with my friends on the ferry to look for ... mines. I think we must have read too many Enid Blyton adventure books, thinking we could save the ships. We must have been nine years old. I realise now that back then we didn't have much fear living through the war days when we were children.
>
> In the early 1960s, my mum was coming home from work one lunchtime on the ferry from the Pier Head to Woodside. She heard some young girls being a little hysterical and crying and she asked: "What's the matter?" They said they had seen The Beatles – whom mum had never heard of, thinking they were talking about some 'Big Beetle' insects ...
> They showed mum these four lads getting their photo taken which was, of course, John, Paul, George and Ringo. Little did she know how famous they would become!

JEAN FURLONG, BEBINGTON

> I MET my husband in 1964. For three years, seven nights a week, we used to get the ferry over from Liverpool to Woodside. We simply loved going back and forth on it. We got to know everyone on the ferry. Down the stairs we used to sit and have a cup of tea and a bacon butty. I had Horlicks sweets. I was addicted to them and he used to bring them to me every night.
> Four years ago it was his 60th birthday and for one of his presents I went down to Woodside and kept taking photos of the ferry until I got the right one. Then I sent it away and had it blown up and put on a canvas – I had the name changed across it and wrote 'Memories are made of this'. It's now on our bedroom wall.

MERSEY MEMORIES

BRIDGET ROBERTS, ANFIELD

LOVE BOAT

Top, hearts torn in every way – romance on the ferry in 1990. Above, Santa Cross the Mersey – ferry crews catch up with the spirit of Christmas in 1988

WOODSIDE FERRY

BIRKENHEAD FERRIES

Farewells and happy returns at Woodside Ferry, 1959

A Bedford van on the floating roadway in November 1960

'Mate' Barry Jones on the bridge of the Royal Iris in 1991

GIANT STEPS

Spring sunshine draws the crowds for a walk along
Liverpool's Landing Stage in April 1960

WALKING ON WATER

Motorists had to use the Mersey Tunnel, but when
Bill Reilly wanted to get to the other side of the
river, he just walked across . . . as part of his job
inspecting the waterpipe lines which crossed the
Mersey in a 784 feet tunnel near Widnes. Bill is
seen here at the tunnel entrance in 1963

Yoko Ono and Sean Lennon on
a visit to Liverpool in the 1980s

STARS OF THE STAGE

The ferries have proved inspirational in the world of television, arts and literature,
and their starring role in popular culture has drawn fans from around the world.

THE ferries have been celebrities in their own 'write.' They appeared in the opening credits of the 60s TV series Liver Birds.

They also appeared in Liver Birds creator Carla Lane's Mersey-based series Bread. You couldn't keep the Boswell clan away from the ferries especially when they wanted to scatter a family member's ashes in the river. The episode was both poignant and hilarious.

And for 20 golden years the ferries would glide across the screen in the opening small-screen credits of Phil Redmond's anarchic soap opera Brookside.

In 2008 they also became the focal point of the Liverpool Nativity BBC drama. Jennifer Ellison, Geoffrey Hughes and a starry crew of Merseysiders put a new slant on a famous Christmas Story.

Celebrities love the boats when they visit the city. Eddie Izzard climbed on board during a trek to Merseyside and Tony Christie was not only a star guest passenger but he performed a special show following his amazing comeback en route to Amarillo where Marie still waits for him.

The ferries have become stage struck, too.

At the Liverpool Empire musicians Ron and Alan Fennah succeeded with a labour of love. They approached writer Helen Forrester about turning her autobiography into a musical. Two Pence to Cross the Mersey, a real harrowing life story of a once, well-to-do family returning to a recession hit Liverpool in the poverty stricken 30s, put the ferries firmly on the theatrical map. A book now studied in schools. The ferries for Helen in her youth became a symbol of hope. A dream weaver . . .

The musical sold out and continues to do so telling its tale of a young woman who dreamt of getting the ferry to a new world . . . just across the water and for just a few pence. Helen recalls in her best seller: "The shore hands were casting off the ferry boat and I looked wistfully across the water at the empty Cammell Laird shipyards in Birkenhead.

"My eyes followed the shore along to the spires of Wallasey."

Happily one day Helen, now based in Canada, did finally get the ferry with her son.

Barbra Streisand filming
Yentl aboard the
Manxman ferry in 1983

THE WRITE STUFF

The ferries became a symbol of hope in Helen
Forrester's best-seller. Below, Nicholas Monsarratt,
Liverpool-born author of The Cruel Sea, contemplates
the river on a spring morning in April 1955

NEW HORIZONS

The world-famous Mersey Ferries are riding the crest of a wave of popularity as the region's most popular paid-for tourism attraction, contributing – with their associated attractions – more than £32m to the local tourism economy and supporting the equivalent of 742 full-time jobs.

IT is a tremendous success story which originates in a decision taken more than a decade ago ago to reposition the Ferries firmly into the tourism economy to secure their long-term financial future.

For more than 800 years the Mersey Ferries plied the commuter route across the Mersey providing a vital commuter link and a crucial link in the chain of history that made Liverpool one of the mightiest sea ports in the world.

But the challenge to their monopoly was gradually eroded by the development of under-river rail and road links. In 1934, when the Queensway Tunnel opened, more than 33 million commuters a year were using the ferries.

In 1970, a year before the Kingsway Tunnel opened, this figure has slumped to around two and a half million passengers a year and for the next three decades the decline continued with the exception of 1964 – the year Gerry Marsden recorded 'Ferry Cross the Mersey'.

The song may have stirred the romantic and the curious to visit the Mersey Ferries but their full potential as a tourist attraction was not exploited until the arrival of Neil Scales as Chief Executive of Merseytravel, which owns and operates the ferries.

Faced with the continuing downward spiral in passenger numbers there was the stark choice of reducing commuter crossings to a loss-making skeletal service or a complete change of course.

SUCCESS STORY

Investment has now included a new £10.5 million state-of-the art terminal at Pier Head. The terminal includes a restaurant with stunning panoramic views across the Mersey, a cafe, gift shop and The Beatles Story, Pier Head

The decision was taken to invest in their future as a tourism attraction while preserving a commuter service.

During the past decade more than £80m has been invested in the ferries and it has paid handsome dividends. The decline was halted and now there are ever increasing passenger numbers.

Four years ago 558,741 passengers used the ferries. Last year the figure was 683,896 of which more than 65 per cent were tourists and 16 per cent of these were from abroad. With tourism playing an increasingly more important role in the region's economy these figures are set to rise.

The investment in the future began with a multimillion pound refurbishment of the three ferries.

The last to be completed was the Woodchurch. She was renamed the Snowdrop after the original Mersey Ferry which was the first vessel to sail down the Manchester Ship Canal in 1893, five months before it was officially opened by Queen Victoria.

Investment has now included a new £10.5 million state-of-the art terminal at Pier Head with major refurbishments and additional attractions at the Seacombe and Woodside terminals providing a unique "tourism triangle" to complement the ever popular River Explorer and Manchester Ship Canal Cruises.

Seacombe Ferry Terminal is now home to Spaceport, the UK's most modern space themed visitor attraction which is housed in a listed building adjacent to the main terminal. It includes a space pod, simulator and planetarium. It is designed to be both educational and entertaining, and is particularly popular with school parties.

Spaceport also hosts visiting exhibitions which have included Dr Who, Wallace and Gromit in Space and 'One Small Step', an exhibition celebrating 40 years since the original lunar landings.

The refurbished terminal building also houses a play area for children including a mini indoor harbour where youngsters can pilot their own radio-controlled ferry boats. The Woodside terminal has been refurbished to revive the splendour of the Victorian age with a restaurant offering unrivalled indoor and outdoor balcony views across the Mersey.

It is also home to the award winning U-Boat Story featuring one of the last four remaining U–boats in the world. It is an exhibition which has captured the imagination of people of all ages. ➤

The centrepiece is U-534 which was saved from an uncertain future by Merseytravel two years ago when its previous berth, the Historic Warships Museum, was closed. Since it opened the U-Boat Story has been a resounding success achieving more than double the number of visitors forecasted in its first year. The U-Boat Story also includes a collection of well-preserved artefacts found on board U-534, including two Enigma machines, plus filmed interviews with survivors, providing a graphic picture of life on board a World War 11 U-boat.

A specially built viewing platform allows visitors to see inside the well preserved U-boat and alongside is one of the three T11 Zaukonig advanced homing torpedoes found on board. These were the most advanced torpedoes in the world at the end of World War 11.

The latest addition to the exhibition will be a full-

CRUISE CONTROL

The Mersey Ferry Snowdrop on the Manchester Ship Canal

size replica conning tower complete with periscope offering panoramic views across the river.

The recently opened Pier Head terminal is one of the most environmentally friendly buildings of its type, designed to complement the Three Graces and Liverpool's waterfront World Heritage status.

It includes a restaurant which offers stunning panoramic views across the Mersey, a cafe, gift shop and The Beatles Story, Pier Head which contains memorabilia of the world's most popular group as well as a 4D cinema. The Beatles Story Pier Head complements the Albert Dock-based Beatles Story exhibition which is also owned by Merseytravel.

A new landing stage at Pier Head, complete with

waiting room, is accessed directly from the terminal building. Pier Head is also the starting point for the 50 minute River Explorer cruises and the Manchester Ship Canal Cruises. The six-hour cruises, which travel the length of the Manchester Ship Canal in each direction, are proving ever more popular with double the number of passengers seen five years ago.

The 35-mile trip – with a licensed bar and refreshments on board – offers unique scenery and a lively commentary telling the story of how this magnificent waterway shaped the city of Manchester and the North West of England.

The cruise includes passing through locks and under bridges that have remained largely unchanged since their construction over 100 years ago.

On most cruises there's also an additional opportunity to enjoy a two and a half hour stopover before returning by bus.

These stopovers allow the chance to visit The Lowry, Imperial War Museum, or Lowry Outlet Mall in Salford Quays; the U-boat Story at Woodside, with its real German WWII U-534 submarine; or Liverpool's central attractions and Albert Dock

This year sees the introduction of Ship Canal Cruises from a new starting point, adjacent to the National Waterways Boat Museum at Ellesmere Port, offering visitors the chance to explore further the story of Britains canals and waterways.

As sure as the River Mersey ebbs and flows the Mersey Ferries and its attractions will continue to adapt to meet the requirements of an ever-increasing tourism market.

Information on all the attractions and sailing times can be found on the Mersey Ferries website: www.merseyferries.co.uk

TWO WORLDS AT WAR

Part of the tour around the German U Boat U-534 at Mersey Ferries Woodside Ferry Terminal, Birkenhead. Mark Dowd, (left) Chairman of Merseytravel, with Chief Executive Neil Scales

GREAT READS FROM THE HEART OF THE CITY

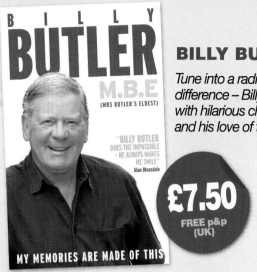

BILLY BUTLER M.B.E.

Tune into a radio show with a difference – Billy's life story, packed with hilarious childhood memories and his love of trivia.

£7.50
FREE p&p
(UK)

Only £2.00
+£1 p&p
(UK)

THE WAY WE WORKED

Unilever, Vernons, Littlewoods, Crawford's, Tate & Lyle, Woolies. Our jobs – our memories.

ECHO LIVERPOOL **DAILY POST**
EXCLUSIVE OFFER

The Liners of Liverpool DVD

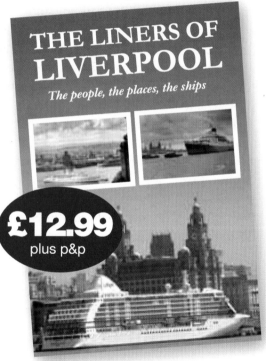

£12.99
plus p&p

Peter Elson guides us through the People, Places and Ships that shaped Liverpool as a cruising port.
Historic footage, images and interviews, including up to date footage of Queen Victoria.
Running time 1 hour.

ON SALE NOW

www.merseyshop.com
or phone **0845 143 0001**

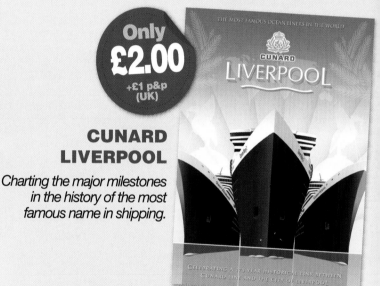

Only £2.00
+£1 p&p
(UK)

CUNARD LIVERPOOL

Charting the major milestones in the history of the most famous name in shipping.

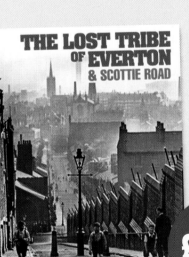

THE LOST TRIBE OF EVERTON & SCOTTIE ROAD

This nostalgic book by Ken Rogers will take you back 'home' into the inner city streets and make you feel proud.

Only £9.99
FREE p&p
(UK)

To order call: 0845 143 0001 or visit MERSEYSHOP.COM

* Offers while stocks last. Prices subject to change.

SCOTTIE ROAD

The bricks and mortar of Scottie Road may be a memory but the spirit lingers on. Featuring great photographs from the Scottie Press collection and rarely seen historical images from the League of Welldoers' Lee Jones Collection.

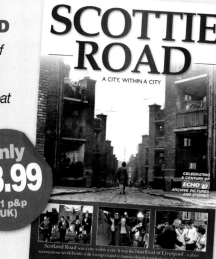

Only £3.99
+£1 p&p (UK)

Only £3.99
+£1 p&p (UK)

LOST CINEMAS OF LIVERPOOL

Book your ticket for a trip down movie memory lane, to a time when Liverpool was a Tinsel Town in its own right and there was a cinema on every corner.

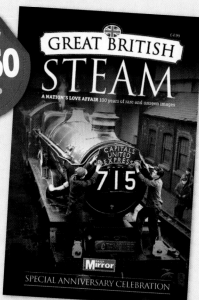

Only £2.50
+£1 p&p (UK)

GREAT BRITISH STEAM

50 years on, this Mirror publication recalls the great steam stories, landmarks, disasters and celebrations from it's magnificent archive.

"Are yer dancin'?"
"Are yer askin'?"

Send us your stories and you could have a starring role in our next archive special...

THERE was a time when gliding and spinning across the dance floor, under glitter balls and subtle lighting in a myriad of famous venues, was THE number one entertainment activity for every adult on Merseyside.

Did you visit places like the Grafton, Locarno, Orrell Park Ballroom, the Rialto, Peppers on Aubrey Street, Blair Hall on Walton Road, or Reece's in the city centre?

Have you got vivid memories of giant venues like the Tower Ballroom in New Brighton, and St George's Hall, or have you got personal dance tales about smaller district venues that have long since drifted out of our psyche? Have you ever been knocked back on the dance floor after asking: "Are yer dancin'?"

Or were you one of those men with two left feet who stood on the fringe of the floor for hours, terrified to cross the line into that seething mass of swaying and rhythmic inter-action?

We want to hear from you as we prepare a fascinating magazine that will bring back some fantastic memories of the real-life 'Strictly Come Dancing' era. Send your stories and pictures to: Peter Grant, Liverpool Daily Post & Echo, Old Hall Street, Liverpool L69 3EB, or email petergrant@liverpoolecho.co.uk